FPL
J597.4

Harcourt
22,83

Electric Eels

By Duncan Scheff

Steadwell Books

Raintree Steck-Vaughn Publishers

A Harcourt Company

Austin · New York

www.raintreesteckvaughn.com

ANIMALS OF THE RAIN FOREST

Published by Raintree Steck-Vaughn Publishers,
an imprint of Steck-Vaughn Company.

Library of Congress Cataloging-in-Publication Data
ISBN: 0-7398-5527-1
Printed and bound in the United States of America
1 2 3 4 5 6 7 8 9 10 WZ 05 04 03 02

Produced by Compass Books

Photo Acknowledgments
Corbis, 22; John Shedd Aquarium/Patrice Ceisel, cover, 8, 15, 19, 28-29; Luiz Claudio
Marigo, 11, 12, 16; Photo Researchers/Tom McHugh, 20; Rob & Ann Simpson, 6, 24, 26;
Tom Stack & Associates/Gary Milburn, title page.

Editor: Bryon Cahill
Consultant: Sean Dolan

Content Consultant
Dr. William Fink, Professor and Curator, Department of Ecology and Evolutionary
Biology, Museum of Zoology, University of Michigan

This book supports the National Science Standards.

Contents

MEXICO

BELIZE
HONDURAS
NICARAGUA
GUATEMALA
EL SALVADOR
*Caribbean
Sea*

COSTA RICA

PANAMA

ECUADOR

COLOMBIA

VENEZUELA

*North
Atlantic
Ocean*

GUYANA
SURINAME

FRENCH
GUIANA
(FRANCE)

ORINOCO
RIVER

AMAZON
RIVER

PERU

BRAZIL

BOLIVIA

*South
Pacific
Ocean*

PARAGUAY

CHILE

*South
Atlantic
Ocean*

ARGENTINA   URUGUAY

Range of the
Electric Eel

Surrounding
Land

Water

Borders

Rivers

N
W   E
S

4

A Quick Look at Electric Eels

What do electric eels look like?

Electric eels have long, thin bodies. They are brown or olive with tan spots. Their undersides are usually lighter. Some electric eels have reddish undersides.

Where do electric eels live?

Electric eels live in warm rivers in the Amazon region of South America. They often may be found in shallow, muddy water.

What do electric eels eat?

Electric eels eat meat. Their main food is fish. They also eat frogs, worms, insects, and other small animals.

Like all electric eels, this one does not have a fin on its back.

Electric Eels in the Rain Forest

Electric eels are among the most unusual animals in the rivers of South America's rain forest. A rain forest is a warm place where many different trees and plants grow close together, and a lot of rain falls. Electric eels look a little like true eels. Eels are long, snake-like, and do not have scales. But electric eels are not true eels.

The scientific name for electric eels is *Electrophorus electricus* (ee-lek-troh-FOR-uhs ee-lek-TRI-kuhs). This name comes from the Latin word for **electricity**. Electric eels can give off electric shocks.

Electric eels are Gymnotiformes (jim-NO-tuh-formz). This name means "naked back." Gymnotiformes are fish that do not have fins on their backs. They also have long, knife-shaped bodies, and they can create and give off electricity.

Electric eels live near rocks and plants in rivers.

Where Do Electric Eels Live?

Electric eels live in the northeastern parts of South America and throughout the Amazon region. The Amazon region includes most of South America's largest rain forest, Amazonia. They live in the Amazon and Orinoco Rivers and other rivers that connect to them.

Electric eels are freshwater fish. Freshwater has little or no salt in it. Oceans are saltwater. Electric eels stay near the edges of rivers, lakes, or ponds. The water there is shallow, still, or slow-flowing. Electric eels usually live near plants and leaf litter. Leaf litter is made up of dead leaves and branches that have fallen into the water.

How Do Electric Eels Breathe?

Electric eels live in warm, muddy water. Because this water has very little oxygen in it, they have had to **adapt** to breathe oxygen in the air. Living things need to breathe oxygen in order to live. Other fish use body parts called **gills** to absorb, or take in, oxygen from water.

Electric eels gather most of their air with organs in their mouths. Electric eels must go to the water's surface about every three minutes to breathe air. They have to go to the surface more often if the water is warm, because there is less oxygen in warm water. They stick their head out of the water and suck in air through their mouth. Air then flows into their mouths and is taken into the body through the lung-like organs there. Electric eels will die in about 20 minutes if they cannot swim to the surface to breathe.

What Do Electric Eels Look Like?

The electric eel is an unusual looking fish. It has a long, thin, snake-like body. Adult electric eels can grow up to 9 feet (3 m) long and weigh up to 50 pounds (23 kg). They have a wide mouth and two small eyes. The eyes are usually blue or green.

Tiny scales cover an electric eel's body. A **scale** is a small, plate-like piece of bone covered with thick skin. The skin on the top side of the body is brown or olive with tan spots. The scales on the bottom side are usually lighter in color. Some electric eels have reddish undersides.

Electric eels have very long tails. About 80 percent of the electric eel's body is made up of the tail. This section contains the electric organs. These body parts are special muscles that create and give off electricity. The electric eel can produce an electrical charge of 600 volts or more. A volt is a measure of the force of an electric charge.

Electric eels do not breathe the way most fish do. They have smaller gills than other fish. They gather only about 25 percent of the air they need with their gills.

You can see the small gill openings of this electric eel.

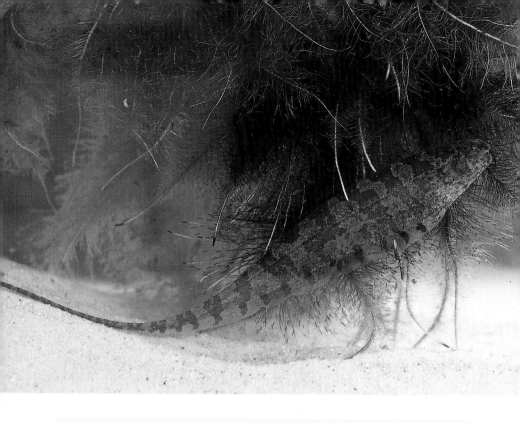

A This is an electric knifefish. It is the
electric eel's closest relative.

How Are Electric Eels Different from True Eels?

Many people do not know that electric eels are not really eels. Electric eels have a body shape like true eels. But electric eels are not closely related to true eels.

True eels belong to a group scientists call Anguilliformes (ahn-GWIL-ih-forms). Electric eels do not belong to this group.

True eels are different from electric eels in other ways, too. Many true eels have a dorsal fin that runs along their back. Electric eels do not have a dorsal fin. True eels have a different life cycle than electric eels. For part of their life, true eels are a thin, almost see-through larva. Electric eels have no such life stage.

Electric eels live in different places than true eels. Most true eels live in ocean waters. But electric eels cannot survive in salty ocean water.

Other Kinds of Electric Fish

There are many kinds of electric fish besides the electric eel. Other electric fish include knifefish, electric catfish, electric rays, and stargazers. The electric eel is the largest electric fish. It also gives off the strongest electric shock.

Knifefish are the electric fish most closely related to electric eels. These long, thin fish also live in the Amazon region. They can grow almost 2 feet (60 cm) long. Most adult knifefish are dark brown or black with light-tan bands that cross their bodies.

How Do Electric Eels Produce Electricity?

The electric eel has special organs that allow it to give off electric charges. The main pair of electric organs runs along the length of the tail. The other two pairs are smaller. They are under the main pair in the electric eel's tail. The electric organs store and release energy like a battery.

Each electric organ has thousands of cells called electroplaques. Each electroplaque makes a weak electric charge. The electric eel can have all of the cells produce a powerful charge at once.

The electric eel has adapted to use its electric organs. It does not swim by moving its tail as other fish do. Moving the tail would make it hard to send and receive electrical signals. Instead, the electric eel has a long anal fin that runs along the entire underside of its body. The eel can move its anal fin to swim forward and backward. Most other fish cannot move their anal fins in this way. They must move their tails to swim.

The electric eel is always sending out electric pulses. It can control whether it sends out strong electric pulses or not. It sends out weak electric

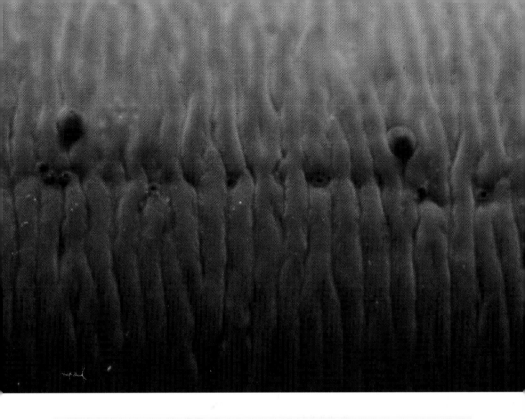

pulses to sense objects around it. It sends out
strong electric pulses to kill **prey** or when it senses
the approach of danger, such as a person or other
large object in the water. Some scientists think
electric eels use electric signals to **communicate**.

Electric eels rest after they produce an electric
charge. Their bodies must make and store more
energy before the electroplaques can work again.

Electric eels eat water beetles like this one that is swimming among water plants.

What Electric Eels Eat

Electric eels are **carnivores**. This means that they eat only meat. Electric eels usually do not eat large prey. Prey is an animal that is hunted as food. But electric eels will eat almost any small creatures that they can catch.

Fish is the most common food of the electric eel. They also hunt shrimp and small animals, such as frogs. They may catch insects like beetles, which swim on top of the water. They may even eat worms or dead animals that they find.

Electric eels are top predators. A **predator** is an animal that hunts another animal for food. Top predators do not have natural enemies. Other animals do not like the strong electric shock that electric eels give off. They usually stay away from the electric eel.

Catching Food

Electric eels have a special way of hunting. They use electric shocks to **stun** or kill prey. To stun is to make something senseless, or unable to react to its surroundings. Repeated shocks from an electric eel can kill an animal as large as a horse. One shock will not kill a person, but several shocks could.

Electric eels cannot see well with their small eyes. In fact, adult electric eels are almost blind. Instead, they use electricity to find prey. To do this, they send pulses of electricity into the dark, muddy water. The pulses create an **electric field** around the electric eel. When an object enters the electric field, the electricity flows around or through it. This affects the electric field.

Special cells on the electric eel's head sense the change in the electric field. This tells the electric eel the size of the object and where it is. In this way, the eel can find prey and move around its home range.

Electric eels are most active early in the morning and in the evening. They do most of their hunting during these periods. To hunt, they usually hide among plants and wait for prey,

▲ **Electric eels hide behind objects, such as plants or fallen logs, to wait for prey.**

such as fish, to swim by. When prey enters the eel's electric field, the electric eel strikes. It releases a powerful pulse of electricity. An electric eel may kill several animals with one charge.

Most prey die quickly. Prey that does not die is stunned. It cannot swim away or fight back. The eel then swallows the prey whole.

Electric eels, like these two, come together only during their mating season.

An Electric Eel's Life Cycle

Electric eels mate during the spring of each year. This time of year is the rainy season in the Amazon region.

Scientists believe electric eels use electric signals to attract mates. Females may send out special signals. The signals tell males that they are ready to mate.

Males and females probably pair off together to mate. The female looks for a good place to lay eggs. She usually hides the eggs under plants or fallen tree logs. She lays several hundred eggs at a time.

The female stays near the eggs. She protects the eggs until they hatch. When the eggs hatch, the female stays in the area.

> **This electric eel is old enough to find its own home range.**

Young Electric Eels

Newly hatched electric eels look like tiny worms. Because they are so small, they cannot produce a strong shock. The electric eel's shock becomes stronger as it gets larger.

Young electric eels face many dangers. Until they are large enough to produce a strong shock, the young electric eels have no way to protect themselves. Many young electric eels are eaten by birds and larger fish. Few live to become adults.

Young electric eels cannot produce enough electricity to kill large prey. So, they do not eat fish. Instead, they eat insect larvae. These young insects live in the water.

Newly hatched electric eels grow quickly. As they grow, they learn to control their electric organs. They learn how to send strong pulses for large prey and weak pulses for smaller prey. Then, they begin to hunt larger prey.

Young electric eels also find their own home range. This is the area where they hunt and spend most of their time. A home range may be in an underwater hole or inside a tree trunk that has fallen into the water.

Electric eels may fight to keep predators and other electric eels from entering their home ranges. During mating season, males often fight other males. Electric eels use electric charges against each other. But the charges are not deadly to other electric eels. An electric eel's body can survive strong electric shocks.

Electric eels will not attack people unless they sense danger.

The Future of Electric Eels

Many rain forest animals are in great danger of dying out. People destroy rain forest areas to build farms and cities. They cut down trees for wood. Thousands of rain forest animals have already died out because of this.

People sometimes use rivers and lakes for transportation. This kills some fish. But electric eels are able to live in areas where people also live.

People in South America know to stay away from electric eels. People do not hunt electric eels for food. Electric eels do not attack people. They send out electric shocks only if they sense danger. Both electric eels and people tend to stay away from one another.

▲ Electric eels will die out if their prey cannot survive changes to the rain forest.

What Will Happen to Electric Eels?

Electric eels may be in danger one day if people continue to destroy the rain forest. The electric eels may be able to survive great changes to the land around them. However, their prey may not survive these changes. Electric eels could be in danger of dying out if they do not have enough prey to eat.

The electric eel can produce a charge that is strong enough to supply the power needed to turn on a roomful of light bulbs.

Electric eels are a restricted species. This means that people cannot own them. Electric eels could be too successful, if released into new areas. Other fish might not be able to compete with electric eels for food.

Scientists have known about the electric eel for more than 200 years. But scientists still know very little about some parts of electric eels' lives. Today, scientists are studying the electric eel. They are learning more about how the eel produces and uses electricity.

Scientists do not know exactly how many electric eels live in the world. But they believe that electric eels will survive. Electric eels can live in water that contains very little oxygen. They can also eat many kinds of prey. These abilities will help electric eels survive in their rain forest homes for many years to come.

small eyes
see page 10

gills
see page 10

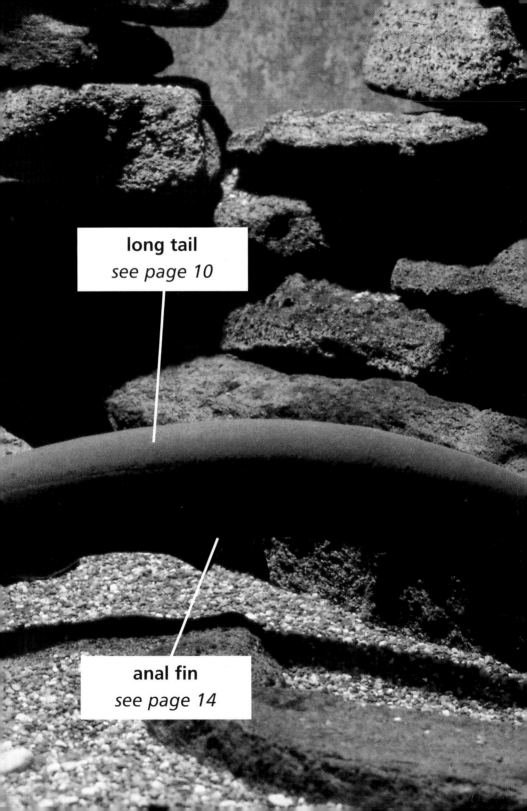

long tail
see page 10

anal fin
see page 14

Glossary

adapt (uh-DAPT)—to change in order to better fit the environment

carnivores (KAHR-nuh-vors)—animals that eat only meat

communicate (kuh-MYOO-nuh-kate)—to share information with each another

electric field (i-LEK-trick FEELD)—an electrically charged area that surrounds an animal or object

electricity (i-lek-TRISS-uh-tee)—a form of energy caused by the movement of protons and electrons, which are tiny parts that make up an atom

gills (GILS)—the organs on a fish's side through which it breathes

predator (PRED-uh-tur)—an animal that hunts other animals for food

prey (PRAY)—an animal hunted as food

scale (SKALE)—a small, plate-like piece of thick skin that covers some animals

stun (STUHN)—to make something senseless, or unable to react to its surroundings

Internet Sites

Enchanted Learning—Electric Eel
www.enchantedlearning.com/subjects/fish/
    printouts/Electriceelprintout.shtml

Journey into Amazonia—Waterworlds
www.pbs.org/journeyintoamazonia/
    waterworlds.html

Useful Address

Fort Worth Zoo
1989 Colonial Parkway
Fort Worth, TX 76110

Books to Read

Arnold, Caroline. *Shockers of the Sea: and Other Electric Animals.* Watertown, MA: Charlesbridge Publishing, 1999.

Landau, Elaine. *Electric Fish.* New York: Children's Press, 1999.

Index